101 BACK TO SCHOOL JOKES

By Lisa Eisenberg and Katy Hall

Illustrated by John DeVore

SCHOLASTIC INC.
New York Toronto London Auckland Sydney

Cover illustration by Robert DeMichiell.

ISBN 0-590-96537-9

Text copyright © 1994 by Katy Hall and Lisa Eisenberg.
Illustrations copyright © 1994 by Scholastic Inc.
All rights reserved. Published by Scholastic Inc.

12 11 10 9 8 7 6 5 4 3   8 9/9 0 1/0

Printed in the U.S.A.   01

First Scholastic printing, August 1994

THE BACK-TO-SCHOOL CLOTHES-OUT!

Pete: Say, don't you think that new shirt Grandma sent you for school is a little tight?

Repete: I can't tell you. I'm too choked up!

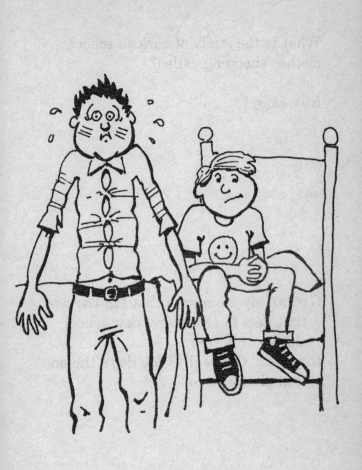

What is the study of back-to-school clothes shopping called?

Buy-ology!

Greta: My mom says that I'm the one that gets to choose my new school clothes this year.
Regreta: Oh, really? My dog's the one that chews mine!

BACK TO GETTING UP BEFORE NOON!

What's the hardest thing about falling out of bed on the first day of school?

The floor!

Mom: Greta, why are you so late getting up on the first day of school?

Greta: My clock was slow.

Mom: Ha! Do you expect me to believe that?

Greta: Of course. You'd be slow, too, if you'd been running all night!

Regreta: I knocked my alarm clock on the floor in the middle of the night.

Greta: What time was it?

Regreta: Time to get a new alarm clock!

Emmie: Mom, I'm not going back to school this year.

Mom: Why not?

Emmie: Because last year the teacher said three plus seven made ten. Then he said five plus five made ten. And then he said eight plus two made ten.

Mom: So?

Emmie: So, I'm not going back till he makes up his mind!

Kathy: Dad, I'm not planning to do any schoolwork this year.

Dad: Why not? Hard work never killed anyone.

Kathy: I know! And I don't plan to be its first victim!

BACK TO A
BRAND-NEW TEACHER!

What's the difference between your new teacher and a train?

Your new teacher says, "Spit out your gum!"; but a train says, "Choo! Choo!"

Why did the new teacher give Smart Alec an A-plus?

Because he made a WISE-crack!

Principal: Timmy, it's only the first day of school, and I've already had a lot of complaints about you from your teachers. What have you been doing?

Timmy: Nothing.

Principal: And that's *exactly* what your teachers said!

Kurt: I spent eight hours over my new spelling book last night.

Teacher: It's wonderful that you spent so much time studying!

Kurt: Who said anything about studying? My spelling book was under my bed when I went to sleep!

BACK TO THE CAFETERI-<u>YUCK</u>

Knock, knock!
Who's there?
Betty!
Betty who?
Betty can't eat that whole plateful of
  tuna noodle casserole!

Knock, knock!
Who's there?
Anita!
Anita who?
Anita nother fifty cents so I can buy
  dessert!

Knock, knock!
Who's there?
Candy!
Candy who?
Candy cafeteria possibly serve something better tomorrow?

BACK TO SCHOOL
WITH YOUR PRINCI-<u>PAL</u>

Principal: So tell me, Mr. Wartman. Is that little Andrew Anderson as hopeless as he was last year?

Teacher: Well, I don't like to say he's hopeless. But he *did* have to cheat to get an F on a test today!

Principal: I've been watching you to-day, Mr. Wartman. It was wonderful how you managed to stay on your toes for the entire first day of school!

Teacher: I had no choice. My students put thumbtacks on my chair!

BACK-TO-SCHOOL DAZE

Mom: How did you like going back to school today, Ben?

Ben: Oh, going was okay. And coming home was all right, too. It was the in-between part I didn't like!

Mom: Jen, why don't you like your new teacher?

Jen: Because she told me to sit at the front for the present. And then she didn't give me any present!

BACK TO THE
SCHOOL PSYCHOLOGIST

Guy: Please, Dr. Mindwarp! I can't go
back to my new classroom. I think
I'm shrinking!

Doc: Well then, Guy, you'll just have to
be a little patient!

Donna: Please, Dr. Mindwarp! I can't go back to my new classroom. I think I'm a pair of curtains!

Doc: Please, Donna! Pull yourself together!

Henry: Please, Dr. Mindwarp! I can't go back to my new classroom. I think I'm a needle!

Doc: Hmmmm. I see your point!

BACK-TO-SCHOOL
BEST-SELLERS

Walking to School on the First Day Back
by Misty Buss

The Day the Car Pool Forgot Me
by I. Rhoda Bike

Can't See the Chalkboard
by Sidney Backrow

*Practical Jokes I Played on the First
    Day of School*
by Major Crackupp

BACK TO SCHOOL
WITH MORE TEACHER'S PESTS

Lenny: My new teacher thinks I'm special.

Mom: How can you tell?

Lenny: She says my behavior puts me in a class of my own!

Mom: Joy, this test score is lower than any of your scores last year.

Joy: I know! And it's all my new teacher's fault!

Mom: Why's that?

Joy: Brainy Billy sat next to me last year. But my new teacher moved him to another seat!

Laura: Mr. Warthog, would you get mad at me for something that I didn't do?

Mr. Warthog: Of course not, Laura.

Laura: Good. Because I didn't do my homework!

MORE BACK-TO-SCHOOL
BEST-SELLERS

*What I Dislike About Returning to
    School*
by Mona Lott

Making It Through the First Week Back
by Gladys Saturday

Is Life Over When Summer Ends?
by Midas Wellbee

BAK TOO SKOOL WITH SPELING

Teacher: How do you spell *cat*, Angela?

Angela: C–A–I —

Teacher: Stop right there. *Cat* doesn't have an I!

Angela: So how does it see to catch a mouse?

Teacher: Melody, spell *mouse*.

Melody: M–O–U–S.

Teacher: But what's at the end of it?

Melody: A tail!

Pete: Ms. Warthog, I've been having a lot of trouble with asthma.

Teacher: Oh, dear. Have you seen the nurse about it?

Pete: I don't *have* it! I just can't spell it!

What happened to the plant on the windowsill of the math classroom?

It grew square roots!

Is a hammer a useful tool in math class?

No, you need multi-pliers!

Teacher: How many feet are in a yard?
Alex: I dunno, Teacher. It all depends on how many people are standing in it!

Kippy: I can remember all my times tables because I have a photographic memory!

Teacher: What a pity it hasn't been developed!

Teacher: If you had six dollars in your left front pocket, and five dollars in your right front pocket, and ten dollars in your back pocket, what would you have?

Lauren: Somebody else's clothes!

Teacher: Who can tell me how many seconds there are in a year?

Eddie: I know! Twelve! January second, February second, March second, April second . . .

BACK TO THE CAFETERI-<u>YUCK</u>, AGAIN!

Quinby: Yuck! There's a bug in my meat loaf!

Cafeteria Worker: Well, take him home and remember — you're not allowed to bring your pets to school.

Prudence: Oh, barf! There's a bug in my milk!

Cafeteria Worker: So *that's* where they go in winter!

Prunella: Arg! There's a bug in my macaroni!

Cafeteria Worker: Don't worry. It won't survive for long in *that* stuff!

Quentin: Ugh! There's a bug in my mashed potatoes!

Cafeteria Worker: They just don't care *what* they eat, do they?

Thorley: Disgusting! There's a bug on my french fries!

Cafeteria Worker: Don't worry, kid. The spider on your hamburger will eat it up in no time!

Thurlow: Gross! There's a bug on my taco!

Cafeteria Worker: Don't worry. How much can one little bug eat anyway?

Thurston: Icky! There's a bug in my carrot cake.
Cafeteria Worker: Of course there is. It's the fly's day off!

Teacher: Who can tell me the shape of the world?

Doug: According to the papers, it's in terrible shape!

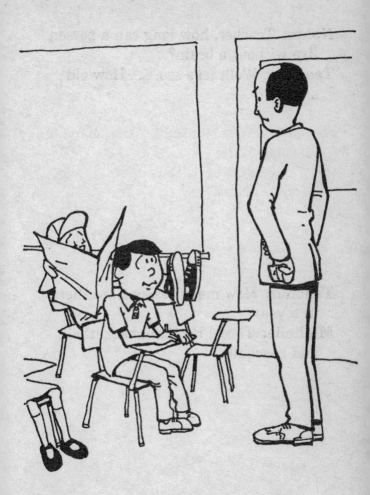

Nolan: Teacher, how long can a person live without a brain?

Teacher: Well, let's see. . . . How old are you?

Teacher: How many seasons are there in a year?

Michelle: Three! Football, basketball, and baseball!

Dad: How is your report card, Pamela?
Pamela: Well, Dad, I decided to do the same thing as George Washington.
Dad: Why, what's that?
Pamela: I went down in history!

Paul: I'm not going to study for history this year.

Mom: Why in the world not?

Paul: I think it's better to let bygones be bygones!

Teacher: Tell me something about the history of the Iron Age.

Patrick: Sorry, but I'm a bit rusty on that one.

Teacher: Where was the Declaration of Independence signed?

Fifi: At the bottom?

Gary: I'm taking ancient history.
Mary: Me, too! Let's get together and talk about old times!

Teacher: What explorer discovered that the world was round?
Lamont: Sir Cumference?

Sir Cumference

Teacher: Where is your pencil, Ludlow?

Ludlow: I ain't got none!

Teacher: Ludlow! Where is your grammar?

Ludlow: She's at her house in Cleveland. And she ain't got my pencil neither!

French Teacher: How do you say *eat* in French?
Bambi: Eat in French!

Teacher: You didn't do too well on this math exam. Your answers were not very good.
Boris: That's okay. Neither were your questions.

Teacher: Jerry, were you copying the answer from your neighbor's paper?
Jerry: Oh, no! I was just checking to see if she had mine right!

Morris: I don't think I deserve a zero on this test!

Teacher: I don't either, but that's the lowest grade I'm allowed to give.

Teacher: When I was your age I could name all the presidents in the proper order.

Sally: Yeah, but when you were my age there'd only been three or four!

BACK TO GYM
(UNLESS YOU HAVE A NOTE!)

When is a basketball player like a baby?

When he dribbles!

Jack: Eeew! Where are you going with that skunk?

Jill: To my gym class.

Jack: But what about the odor?

Jill: Oh, he'll get used to it.

Coach: I can't believe you just threw the basketball right into the swimming pool!

Matt: But, Coach! You told me to sink it!

What did the soccer ball say to the center forward?

"I get a kick out of you!"

EVEN MORE BACK-TO-SCHOOL BEST-SELLERS

What I Love About Returning to School
by I. M. Kidding

Will Jimmy Finally Graduate?
by I. Betty Wont

What Happens When You Get Caught
  Skipping School
by U. Will Gettitt

Why did the students throw eggs at the new drama teacher?

Because eggs go so well with ham!

How are tough teachers like umpires?

They both penalize you for errors!

What can you pay your new teacher even if you're totally broke?

Attention!

What kind of teachers do you find at the South Pole?

Cold ones.

History Teacher: What did the flag
say to the father of our country?
Wilma: Nothing. It just waved.

History Teacher: What did George
Washington do when his hatchet
broke?
Jennifer: He put a new one on his
chopping list!

History Teacher: How did George Washington get his wig?

Jesse: He had it delivered by hair mail!

History Teacher: Why didn't George Washington need a bed?

Devon: Because he'd never lie!

History Teacher: Why were George Washington's troops so tired on April first?

Kevin: They'd just had a March of thirty-one days!

Substitute History Teacher: What did George Washington think of Betsy Ross?

Lori: I give up!

Substitute History Teacher: He thought she was an old sew-and-sew!

Substitute History Teacher: Which president had the sharpest teeth?

Steve: I don't know!

Substitute History Teacher: Jaws Washington!

Substitute History Teacher: Did George Washington ever fight bear?

Sammy: I have no idea.

Substitute History Teacher: No! He always fought with his clothes on!

Teacher: Dorley, please give me the
definition of *autobiography*.
Dorley: A car's life story!

Teacher: Class, you have thirty minutes to write a composition on the subject of baseball.

Jonah: Here's my paper.

Teacher: Why, Jonah, you only spent one minute writing your essay. Let's see what you wrote.

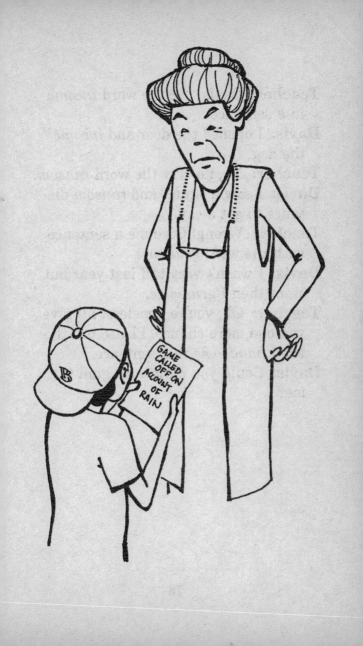

Teacher: Davis, use the word *income* in a sentence.

Davis: I opened the door and *income* the dog.

Teacher: No, no. Try the word *ransom*.

Davis: I saw a skunk and *ransom* distance to get away.

Teacher: Wrong! Give me a sentence with the word *gruesome*.

Davis: I wasn't very tall last year but since then I *gruesome*.

Teacher: Oh, you're hopeless! I'll give you one more chance. Please use the word *handsome* in a sentence.

Davis: Could you *handsome* gum to me?

Teacher: Farley, please give me the definition of *bacteria*.

Farley: The back entrance to the cafeteria!

Teacher: Harley, please give me the definition of *climate*.

Harley: What kids do when they see a tree!

NO! NO! I WON'T GO . . .
BACK TO THE CAFETERI-<u>YUCK</u>!

Kelly: I'm so hungry today I could eat a horse!

Cafeteria Worker: Well, you certainly came to the right place!

Donna: Eeeew! What's this fly doing on my Jell-O?

Cafeteria Worker: Looks to me like back flips!

Steve: What kind of stew is this?
Cafeteria Worker: Rabbit stew — you can tell by all the hares in it!

Andrea: How did you learn to make this pasta?
Cafeteria Worker: I just used my noodle.

Kelly: Are you serving crabs today?
Cafeteria Worker: Pick up a tray! We serve anybody!

Veronica: Oh, Ms. Hypo! Something terrible is happening! My hair is falling out! What can you give me to keep it in?

Nurse: A paper bag.

Hilary: Ms. Hypo, that ointment you gave me makes my arm smart.

Nurse: In that case, rub some on your head!

Della: Ms. Hypo, are the school lunches healthy?

Nurse: I've never heard one complain.

Science Teacher: The law of gravity keeps us from falling off the earth.

Jason: What kept us from falling off before the law was passed?

Science Teacher: But, Tanya, why don't you want to come on our field trip to study insects?

Tanya: Because they bug me!

Science Teacher: What can you tell me about nitrates?

Debby: When you call long distance, they're cheaper than day rates!

BACK TO <u>MU-SICK</u> CLASS

How does the new music teacher brush
his teeth?

With a tuba toothpaste!

Band Student: Our school band played Beethoven last night.
Gym Student: Who won?

How did the new music teacher get locked out of his classroom?

His keys were inside the piano!